Little People, BIG DREAMS™
AUDREY HEPBURN

Written by
Maria Isabel Sánchez Vegara

Illustrated by
Amaia Arrazola

Frances Lincoln
Children's Books

Little Audrey lived in a town called Arnhem, in the Netherlands. She dreamed of what she would do when she grew up . . . Would she become a ballerina—or maybe an actress?

But one day, on her way to ballet class, Audrey saw soldiers on the streets. War had broken out. She watched many families being sent away from their homes—including children just like her.

It was a hard time for Audrey and all the other children. There was very little food, and they were often hungry. Audrey became very ill.

At last the fighting ended, and Audrey moved to London to study dance. Her teacher said she was too weak from the war to become a ballerina. But Audrey didn't give up . . .

She decided to act and dance in musicals instead!

Before long, she was making her first Hollywood film—driving around Rome with the famous actor Gregory Peck!

Every role she played was different from the one before.
One day she was a nun, and the next . . . a princess!

She had a simple rule for life: "Dance as though no one is watching. Sing as though no one can hear you. Live as though heaven is on Earth."

She also liked to spend time alone in her apartment. Every day at breakfast, she read letters from her fans. She was loved by millions of people around the world!

Audrey won award after award. But she worried that she didn't deserve them. While she was a Hollywood star who seemed to have everything . . .

. . . she never forgot that there were children in the world who were hungry, just like she had been.

One day, a charity offered her a new role. They asked her to become their official ambassador and visit children all over the world! So Audrey traveled to India . . .

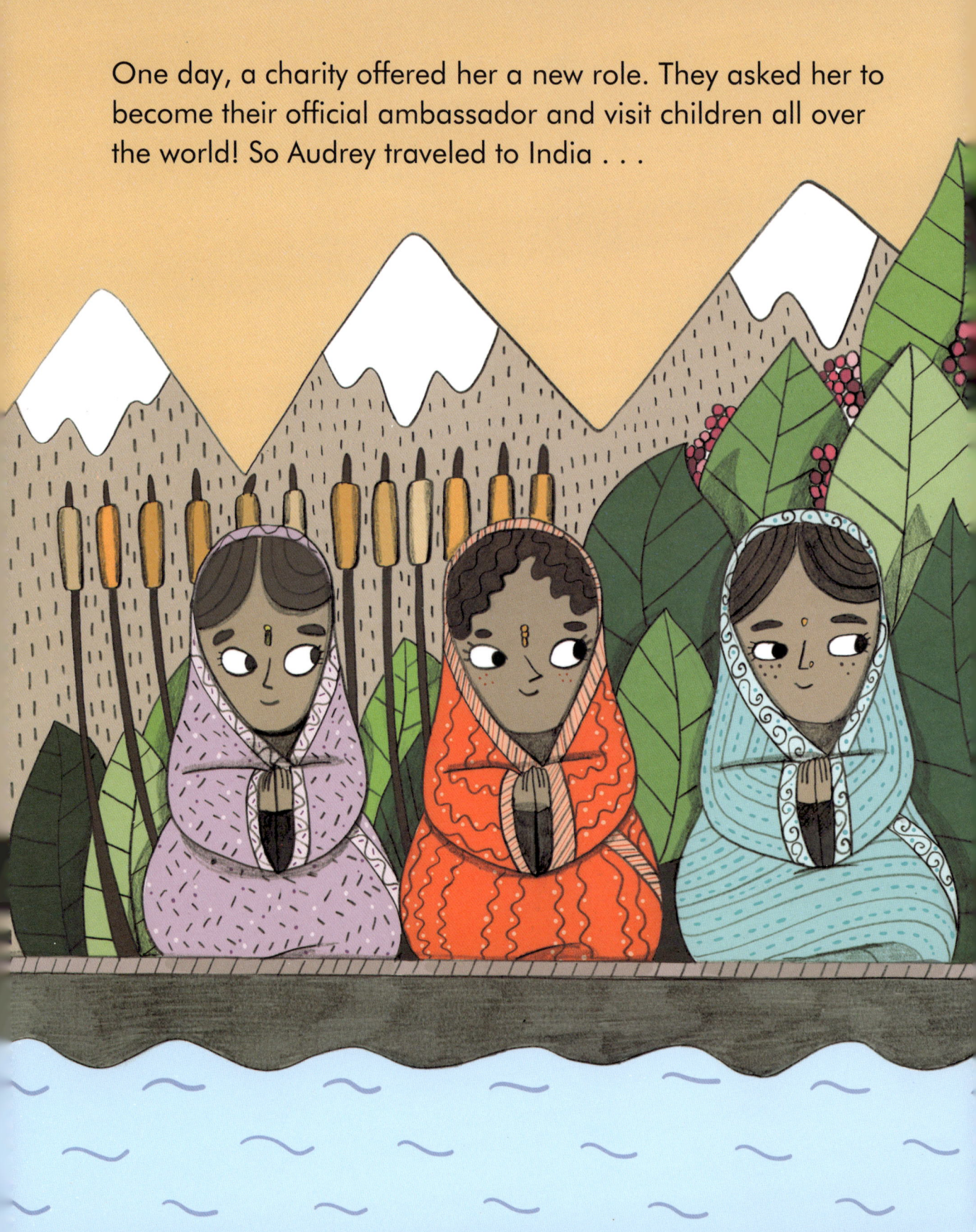

. . . and to Africa! Wherever she went, Audrey tried to make every child happy. She helped raise money to provide children with water, food, and medicine.

Audrey spent the rest of her life helping people across the globe. And that made her happier than acting or dancing ever had.

AUDREY HEPBURN

(Born 1929 • Died 1993)

1946 (right)

1950

Audrey Hepburn was one of the most iconic actresses of stage and screen. She was born Audrey Kathleen Ruston in Belgium in 1929. Her mother, Ella van Heemstra, was a Dutch baroness and her father, Joseph Ruston, was British. Her parents broke up when she was three, and Audrey moved with her mother to Arnhem, a small town in the Netherlands. It was here that Audrey started to take ballet lessons. When World War Two broke out in 1939, Audrey's mother hoped that the Netherlands would be safe. Unfortunately Audrey's family, like many others, suffered greatly during the war. Food was scarce, and she witnessed crimes she would remember for the rest of her life.

1956

1991

After the war, Audrey trained to be a ballerina, moving to London to study at the famous Rambert School of Ballet. But she was weak from years of malnutrition, so she decided to focus on acting instead of ballet. She got her big break in the Broadway play *Gigi*, and went on to star in many Hollywood films, such as *Breakfast at Tiffany's*, winning prestigious awards. During her retirement, the children's charity UNICEF asked her to be their Goodwill Ambassador. She traveled all around the world, raising awareness for children who needed food, clean water, and medicine. Audrey did whatever she could to help others, because she remembered how she had felt when she was a child in need.

Want to find out more about **Audrey Hepburn**?

Have a read of this great book:

Just Being Audrey by Margaret Cardillo

You could also watch one of her many films, such as *My Fair Lady*
or *Roman Holiday*.

Brimming with creative inspiration, how-to projects, and useful information to enrich your everyday life, Quarto Knows is a favourite destination for those pursuing their interests and passions. Visit our site and dig deeper with our books into your area of interest: Quarto Creates, Quarto Cooks, Quarto Homes, Quarto Lives, Quarto Drives, Quarto Explores, Quarto Gifts, or Quarto Kids.

Text copyright © 2015 Maria Isabel Sánchez Vegara. Illustrations copyright © 2015 Amaia Arrazola.
Original concept of the series by Maria Isabel Sánchez Vegara, published by Alba Editorial, s.l.u
Produced under trademark licence from Alba Editorial s.l.u and Beautifool Couple S.L.

First published in the USA in 2017 by Frances Lincoln Children's Books.
This gift box set edition first published in the USA by Lincoln Children's Books,
an imprint of The Quarto Group,
100 Cummings Center, Suite 265D, Beverly, MA 01915, USA.
T +1 978-282-9590 F +1 078-283-2742 QuartoKnows.com

Visit our blogs at QuartoKids.com

First published in Spain in 2015 under the title *Pequeña & Grande Audrey Hepburn*
by Alba Editorial, s.l.u., Baixada de Sant Miquel, 1, 08002 Barcelona
www.albaeditorial.es

All rights reserved.

No part of this publication may be reproduced, stored in a retrieval system, or transmitted,
in any form, or by any means, electrical, mechanical, photocopying, recording or otherwise without the prior
written permission of the publisher or a license permitting restricted copying.

ISBN 978-1-78603-428-1

Published by Rachel Williams • Designed by Karissa Santos
Edited by Katy Flint • Production by Kate O'Riordan

Manufactured in Guangdong, China CC112021

Photographic acknowledgments (pages 28–29, from left to right) 1. Audrey Hepburn with mother, 1946 © Hulton Archive, Getty Images 2. Audrey Hepburn rehearsing at the barre, 1950 © Silver Screen Collection, Getty Images 3. Audrey Hepburn in Funny Face, 1956 © Mondadori Portfolio, Getty Images 4. UNICEF Gala honoring Audrey Hepburn, 1991 © Ron Galella, Getty Images

Collect the Little People, BIG DREAMS™ series:

FRIDA KAHLO	COCO CHANEL	MAYA ANGELOU	AMELIA EARHART	AGATHA CHRISTIE	MARIE CURIE	ROSA PARKS	AUDREY HEPBURN
EMMELINE PANKHURST	ELLA FITZGERALD	ADA LOVELACE	JANE AUSTEN	GEORGIA O'KEEFFE	HARRIET TUBMAN	ANNE FRANK	MOTHER TERESA
JOSEPHINE BAKER	L. M. MONTGOMERY	JANE GOODALL	SIMONE DE BEAUVOIR	MUHAMMAD ALI	STEPHEN HAWKING	MARIA MONTESSORI	VIVIENNE WESTWOOD
MAHATMA GANDHI	DAVID BOWIE	WILMA RUDOLPH	DOLLY PARTON	BRUCE LEE	RUDOLF NUREYEV	ZAHA HADID	MARY SHELLEY
MARTIN LUTHER KING JR.	DAVID ATTENBOROUGH	ASTRID LINDGREN	EVONNE GOOLAGONG	BOB DYLAN	ALAN TURING	BILLIE JEAN KING	GRETA THUNBERG
JESSE OWENS	JEAN-MICHEL BASQUIAT	ARETHA FRANKLIN	CORAZON AQUINO	PELÉ	ERNEST SHACKLETON	STEVE JOBS	AYRTON SENNA
LOUISE BOURGEOIS	ELTON JOHN	JOHN LENNON	PRINCE	CHARLES DARWIN	CAPTAIN TOM MOORE	HANS CHRISTIAN ANDERSEN	STEVIE WONDER

MEGAN RAPINOE	MARY ANNING	MALALA YOUSAFZAI	ANDY WARHOL	RUPAUL	MICHELLE OBAMA	MINDY KALING	IRIS APFEL

ROSALIND FRANKLIN	RUTH BADER GINSBURG	MARILYN MONROE	KAMALA HARRIS	ALBERT EINSTEIN	CHARLES DICKENS	YOKO ONO	MICHAEL JORDAN

NELSON MANDELA	PABLO PICASSO	AMANDA GORMAN	GLORIA STEINEM	FLORENCE NIGHTINGALE	HARRY HOUDINI	J.R.R. TOLKIEN

ACTIVITY BOOKS

STICKER ACTIVITY BOOK	COLORING BOOK	LITTLE ME, BIG DREAMS JOURNAL

Discover more about the series at www.littlepeoplebigdreams.com